Word Scramble Puzzle Book for Adults

This Activity Book belongs to:

....

ANIMALS ARE COOL

PEA   _ _ _

EHESP   _ _ _ _ _

GDO   _ _ _

GIRADTPER   _ _ _ _ _ _ _ _ _

GDHHEGOE   _ _ _ _ _ _ _ _

WCO   _ _ _

IPERSD   _ _ _ _ _ _

LUTERT   _ _ _ _ _ _

TLIOGAARL   _ _ _ _ _ _ _ _ _

ASOHSERE   _ _ _ _ _ _ _ _

LUETRT   _ _ _ _ _ _

ALAML   _ _ _ _ _

BEACHES

ASE   _ _ _

EAS TRSA   _ _ _ _ _ _ _ _

LLGUASE   _ _ _ _ _ _ _

ELSLHSAE   _ _ _ _ _ _ _ _

OSEHRSSEA   _ _ _ _ _ _ _ _ _

RSKAH   _ _ _ _ _

LLSHE   _ _ _ _ _

IPHS   _ _ _ _

HERSO   _ _ _ _ _

ORSSEDHBIR   _ _ _ _ _ _ _ _ _ _

NSSKAC   _ _ _ _ _ _

ORSLNKE   _ _ _ _ _ _ _

BUGS

NEUJ GBU   _ _ _ _ _ _ _

TDDAYIK   _ _ _ _ _ _ _

NSGSIIK UGB   _ _ _ _ _ _ _ _ _ _ _

EINWGCAL   _ _ _ _ _ _ _ _

ULYBDAG   _ _ _ _ _ _ _

RAVLA   _ _ _ _ _

PRLOAEHEPF   _ _ _ _ _ _ _ _ _ _

IELC   _ _ _ _

OTSULC   _ _ _ _ _ _

ESLUO   _ _ _ _ _

NAUL HMOT   _ _ _ _ _ _ _ _ _ _

OGAMTG   _ _ _ _ _ _

CHRISTMAS TIME

IPSTIR
_ _ _ _ _ _

ENIGLJ SLEBL
_ _ _ _ _ _ _ _ _ _ _

ACINMNON
_ _ _ _ _ _ _ _

EAMRNG
_ _ _ _ _ _

NSOLAWBL
_ _ _ _ _ _ _ _

TCSODENROIA
_ _ _ _ _ _ _ _ _ _ _

LNEGA
_ _ _ _ _

EFSWKNOAL
_ _ _ _ _ _ _ _ _

YCEMNHI
_ _ _ _ _ _ _

KCJA OFSRT
_ _ _ _ _ _ _ _ _ _

NSTAI CKNI
_ _ _ _ _ _ _ _ _

PLHRDUO
_ _ _ _ _ _ _

FEELINGS

IMTAENLBAV

_ _ _ _ _ _ _ _ _ _

SNOXIUA

_ _ _ _ _ _ _

ALHFBUS

_ _ _ _ _ _ _

DDACIN

_ _ _ _ _ _

UCTAUIOS

_ _ _ _ _ _ _ _

RFREIHIDO

_ _ _ _ _ _ _ _ _

LEETIILTNGN

_ _ _ _ _ _ _ _ _ _ _

STUMSEORIY

_ _ _ _ _ _ _ _ _ _

IGRCAPATM

_ _ _ _ _ _ _ _ _

LTICLPIAO

_ _ _ _ _ _ _ _ _

LQZAZCUII

_ _ _ _ _ _ _ _ _

UELIGOISR

_ _ _ _ _ _ _ _ _

FOOD

REAP   _ _ _ _

NBOCA   _ _ _ _ _

IHSUS   _ _ _ _ _

INBAKG ADSO   _ _ _ _ _ _ _ _ _ _ _

UTEFBF   _ _ _ _ _ _

TBL   _ _ _

IANNNCOM   _ _ _ _ _ _ _ _

ORLSL   _ _ _ _ _

ARACIV   _ _ _ _ _ _

LBGAE   _ _ _ _ _

FEBE   _ _ _ _

RKPO   _ _ _ _

HALLOWEEN

ROBOLLED

_ _ _ _ _ _ _ _

IWCTH

_ _ _ _ _

TABS

_ _ _ _

ECMOSTU

_ _ _ _ _ _ _

TUAMUN

_ _ _ _ _ _

NKSLTEOE

_ _ _ _ _ _ _ _

TESESW

_ _ _ _ _ _

CAERORSCW

_ _ _ _ _ _ _ _ _

YCAND

_ _ _ _ _

NKFSNETANRIE

_ _ _ _ _ _ _ _ _ _ _ _

YDNCA ONRC

_ _ _ _ _ _ _ _ _

AYH DERI

_ _ _ _ _ _ _ _

IN MY HOUSE

OHSE

_ _ _ _

IEPCS ARCK

_ _ _ _ _ _ _ _ _ _

LITQU

_ _ _ _ _

ALSRETP

_ _ _ _ _ _ _

EARAMC

_ _ _ _ _ _

SDSRE

_ _ _ _ _

THSIR

_ _ _ _ _

WATESRE

_ _ _ _ _ _ _

LCEL HOEPN

_ _ _ _ _ _ _ _ _ _ _

EBRLLAUM

_ _ _ _ _ _ _ _

NIOOLT

_ _ _ _ _ _

WOLET

_ _ _ _ _

IT'S FALL YALL

CESWCAORR   _ _ _ _ _ _ _ _ __

ASETERW   _ _ _ _ _ _ _

NROC   _ _ _ _

EOBMRNEV   _ _ _ _ _ _ _ _

UCABTEAKRRQ   _ _ _ _ _ _ _ _ _ __

NUCIRCNHG   _ _ _ _ _ _ _ __

AVSELE   _ _ _ _ _ _

KAEJTC   _ _ _ _ _ _

SCLDO   _ _ _ _ _

RNGIATMOI   _ _ _ _ _ _ _ __

OBFATOLL   _ _ _ _ _ _ _ _

EWLYLO   _ _ _ _ _ _

ART

ALLDBA   _ _ _ _ _ _

ICTOSUCALA   _ _ _ _ _ _ _ _ _ _

HRCIO   _ _ _ _ _

OCRNTCE   _ _ _ _ _ _ _

NHYSMOCPI   _ _ _ _ _ _ _ _ _

MSNEEEBL   _ _ _ _ _ _ _ _

ULRAA   _ _ _ _ _

RYNHMOA   _ _ _ _ _ _ _

AINLEF   _ _ _ _ _ _

TIAMDARC   _ _ _ _ _ _ _ _

NBDA   _ _ _ _

RESHROTCLA   _ _ _ _ _ _ _ _ _ _

MUSICAL TERMS

RNGISE

_ _ _ _ _ _

GSON

_ _ _ _

RSAOOPN

_ _ _ _ _ _ _

POMET

_ _ _ _ _

ORTEN

_ _ _ _ _

OROMETBN

_ _ _ _ _ _ _ _

MRPTETU

_ _ _ _ _ _ _

UTBA

_ _ _ _

NEUT

_ _ _ _

OVLIA

_ _ _ _ _

LIONIV

_ _ _ _ _ _

PENHOYLOX

_ _ _ _ _ _ _ _ _

LABRADORS

CAK   _ _ _

YGALTII   _ _ _ _ _ _

SNISAACTSE OGD   _ _ _ _ _ _ _ _ _ _ _ _

OELDBN   _ _ _ _ _ _

LLEWYO   _ _ _ _ _ _

KBCLA   _ _ _ _ _

AOOCEHTCL   _ _ _ _ _ _ _ _ _

UPPPY   _ _ _ _ _

NCAIEN   _ _ _ _ _ _

9K   _ _

RFUO EDEGGL   _ _ _ _ _ _ _ _ _ _ _

DOIF   _ _ _ _

LET'S GO

IOVMES

_ _ _ _ _ _

GNKIIH

_ _ _ _ _ _

LORLTS

_ _ _ _ _ _

RRFBUSO

_ _ _ _ _ _ _ _ _ _

DA
IMTE FOF

_ _ _ _ _ _ _ _ _

GSMNWIMI OOLP

_ _ _ _ _ _ _ _ _ _ _ _ _

IBRD TIAGWHNC

_ _ _ _ _ _ _ _ _ _ _ _

ADYOARWB

_ _ _ _ _ _ _ _

SCBUIRONAL

_ _ _ _ _ _ _ _ _ _

GPIPNOSH

_ _ _ _ _ _ _ _

EMOR

_ _ _ _

WNOS EOCN

_ _ _ _ _ _ _ _ _

MID-FALL

KHIGNI

_ _ _ _ _ _

RECOSC

_ _ _ _ _ _

IAOGEFL

_ _ _ _ _ _ _

AKRE

_ _ _ _

ACTECOLOH

_ _ _ _ _ _ _ _ _

CCBPAKAK

_ _ _ _ _ _ _ _

TTHISRSASWE

_ _ _ _ _ _ _ _ _ _ _

TSVREAH

_ _ _ _ _ _ _

UMPPIKN

_ _ _ _ _ _ _

PALPE EPI

_ _ _ _ _ _ _ _ _

ESALPP

_ _ _ _ _ _

ERDIHYA

_ _ _ _ _ _ _

CREATURES

OGDNAR　　　　　　　_ _ _ _ _ _

EBUL LEWAH　　　　_ _ _ _ _ _ _ _ _

ENAYH　　　　　　　_ _ _ _ _

NRUNICO　　　　　　_ _ _ _ _ _ _

NTUA　　　　　　　　_ _ _ _

LUYTPASP　　　　　　_ _ _ _ _ _ _ _

STBASE　　　　　　　_ _ _ _ _ _

DNHUO　　　　　　　_ _ _ _ _

MISHPR　　　　　　　_ _ _ _ _ _

KUSKN　　　　　　　_ _ _ _ _

OLDGULB　　　　　　_ _ _ _ _ _ _

DGALUYB　　　　　　_ _ _ _ _ _ _

POSITIVITY

ELRAEAEGB

_ _ _ _ _ _ _ _ __

ETANAIMD

_ _ _ _ _ _ _ _

IRTGHB

_ _ _ _ _ _

ERELVC

_ _ _ _ _ _

UNGECIRAGON

_ _ _ _ _ _ _ _ _ ___

HESFR

_ _ _ _ _

ELETGN

_ _ _ _ _ _

EUHPOFL

_ _ _ _ _ _ _

IDKN

_ _ _ _

VNILGO

_ _ _ _ _ _

PNOE

_ _ _ _

SAEEDPL

_ _ _ _ _ _ _

SCARY STUFF

LNLAWEHOE
_ _ _ _ _ _ _ _ _

YRCSA
_ _ _ _ _

-KNJLATOECR-AN
_ _ _ _ _ _ _ _ _ _ _ _

TUDHNEA EHUSO
_ _ _ _ _ _ _ _ _ _ _

OSGHT YTOSR
_ _ _ _ _ _ _ _ _ _

IRSEPD
_ _ _ _ _ _

RLWEFOEW
_ _ _ _ _ _ _ _

ARCSY SEMOIV
_ _ _ _ _ _ _ _ _ _ _

DAVERRGYA
_ _ _ _ _ _ _ _ _

INPMPUK
_ _ _ _ _ _ _

MAIPEVR
_ _ _ _ _ _ _

HMRAOMASWLL
_ _ _ _ _ _ _ _ _ _ _

SO BEAUTIFUL

ENIF

_ _ _ _

YXFO

_ _ _ _

IGOOOLDNG-OK

_ _ _ _ _ _ _ _ _ _ _ _ _

OGRSEUGO

_ _ _ _ _ _ _ _

RLFEAUGC

_ _ _ _ _ _ _ _

RANDG

_ _ _ _ _

AMNOEDHS

_ _ _ _ _ _ _ _

THO

_ _ _

YVOLEL

_ _ _ _ _ _

EMTNAFGICNI

_ _ _ _ _ _ _ _ _ _ _

UMEASRVLO

_ _ _ _ _ _ _ _ _

NTDRAAI

_ _ _ _ _ _ _

THANKSGIVING

YAMFLI

_ _ _ _ _ _

OINOCUPCRA

_ _ _ _ _ _ _ _ _ _

RSVETHA

_ _ _ _ _ _ _

LTLOFBOA

_ _ _ _ _ _ _ _

AHSQUS

_ _ _ _ _ _

OCIONKG

_ _ _ _ _ _ _

TIEGAN

_ _ _ _ _ _

RCON

_ _ _ _

ELABT

_ _ _ _ _

YRVGA

_ _ _ _ _

RRENRAYBC

_ _ _ _ _ _ _ _ _

GRMSLIIP

_ _ _ _ _ _ _ _

WATERS

OAYORR   _ _ _ _ _ _

ASINB   _ _ _ _ _

YBA   _ _ _

YOUAB   _ _ _ _ _

EBDN   _ _ _ _

HIBTG   _ _ _ _ _

GBNOLBILA   _ _ _ _ _ _ _ _ _

OGB   _ _ _

ROBOK   _ _ _ _ _

LCAAN   _ _ _ _ _

AACTARCT   _ _ _ _ _ _ _ _

ALNENCH   _ _ _ _ _ _ _

ANIMALS ARE COOL

PEA	=	APE
EHESP	=	SHEEP
GDO	=	DOG
GIRADTPER	=	PARTRIDGE
GDHHEGOE	=	HEDGEHOG
WCO	=	COW
IPERSD	=	SPIDER
LUTERT	=	TURTLE
TLIOGAARL	=	ALLIGATOR
ASOHSERE	=	SEAHORSE
LUETRT	=	TURTLE
ALAML	=	LLAMA

BEACHES

ASE	=	SEA
EAS TRSA	=	SEA STAR
LLGUASE	=	SEAGULL
ELSLHSAE	=	SEASHELL
OSEHRSSEA	=	SEASHORES
RSKAH	=	SHARK
LLSHE	=	SHELL
IPHS	=	SHIP
HERSO	=	SHORE
ORSSEDHBIR	=	SHOREBIRDS
NSSKAC	=	SNACKS
ORSLNKE	=	SNORKEL

BUGS

NEUJ GBU	=	JUNE BUG
TDDAYIK	=	KATYDID
NSGSIIK UGB	=	KISSING BUG
EINWGCAL	=	LACEWING
ULYBDAG	=	LADYBUG
RAVLA	=	LARVA
PRLOAEHEPF	=	LEAFHOPPER
IELC	=	LICE
OTSULC	=	LOCUST
ESLUO	=	LOUSE
NAUL HMOT	=	LUNA MOTH
OGAMTG	=	MAGGOT

CHRISTMAS TIME

IPSTIR	=	SPIRIT
ENIGLJ SLEBL	=	JINGLE BELLS
ACINMNON	=	CINNAMON
EAMRNG	=	MANGER
NSOLAWBL	=	SNOWBALL
TCSODENROIA	=	DECORATIONS
LNEGA	=	ANGEL
EFSWKNOAL	=	SNOWFLAKE
YCEMNHI	=	CHIMNEY
KCJA OFSRT	=	JACK FROST
NSTAI CKNI	=	SAINT NICK
PLHRDUO	=	RUDOLPH

FEELINGS

IMTAENLBAV	=	AMBIVALENT
SNOXIUA	=	ANXIOUS
ALHFBUS	=	BASHFUL
DDACIN	=	CANDID
UCTAUIOS	=	CAUTIOUS
RFREIHIDO	=	HORRIFIED
LEETIILTNGN	=	INTELLIGENT
STUMSEORIY	=	MYSTERIOUS
IGRCAPATM	=	PRAGMATIC
LTICLPIAO	=	POLITICAL
LQZAZCUII	=	QUIZZICAL
UELIGOISR	=	RELIGIOUS

FOOD

REAP	=	PEAR
NBOCA	=	BACON
IHSUS	=	SUSHI
INBAKG ADSO	=	BAKING SODA
UTEFBF	=	BUFFET
TBL	=	BLT
IANNNCOM	=	CINNAMON
ORLSL	=	ROLLS
ARACIV	=	CAVIAR
LBGAE	=	BAGEL
FEBE	=	BEEF
RKPO	=	PORK

HALLOWEEN

ROBOLLED	=	DOORBELL
IWCTH	=	WITCH
TABS	=	BATS
ECMOSTU	=	COSTUME
TUAMUN	=	AUTUMN
NKSLTEOE	=	SKELETON
TESESW	=	SWEETS
CAERORSCW	=	SCARECROW
YCAND	=	CANDY
NKFSNETANRIE	=	FRANKENSTEIN
YDNCA ONRC	=	CANDY CORN
AYH DERI	=	HAY RIDE

IN MY HOUSE

OHSE	=	HOSE
IEPCS	=	SPICE RACK
ARCK		
LITQU	=	QUILT
ALSRETP	=	STAPLER
EARAMC	=	CAMERA
SDSRE	=	DRESS
THSIR	=	SHIRT
WATESRE	=	SWEATER
LCEL HOEPN	=	CELL PHONE
EBRLLAUM	=	UMBRELLA
NIOOLT	=	LOTION
WOLET	=	TOWEL

IT'S FALL YALL

CESWCAORR	=	SCARECROW
ASETERW	=	SWEATER
NROC	=	CORN
EOBMRNEV	=	NOVEMBER
UCABTEAKRRQ	=	QUARTERBACK
NUCIRCNHG	=	CRUNCHING
AVSELE	=	LEAVES
KAEJTC	=	JACKET
SCLDO	=	COLDS
RNGIATMOI	=	MIGRATION
OBFATOLL	=	FOOTBALL
EWLYLO	=	YELLOW

ART

ALLDBA	=	BALLAD
ICTOSUCALA	=	ACOUSTICAL
HRCIO	=	CHOIR
OCRNTCE	=	CONCERT
NHYSMOCPI	=	SYMPHONIC
MSNEEEBL	=	ENSEMBLE
ULRAA	=	AURAL
RYNHMOA	=	HARMONY
AINLEF	=	FINALE
TIAMDARC	=	DRAMATIC
NBDA	=	BAND
RESHROTCLA	=	ORCHESTRAL

MUSICAL TERMS

RNGISE = SINGER

GSON = SONG

RSAOOPN = SOPRANO

POMET = TEMPO

ORTEN = TENOR

OROMETBN = TROMBONE

MRPTETU = TRUMPET

UTBA = TUBA

NEUT = TUNE

OVLIA = VIOLA

LIONIV = VIOLIN

PENHOYLOX = XYLOPHONE

LABRADORS

CAK	=	AKC
YGALTII	=	AGILITY
SNISAACTSE OGD	=	ASSISTANCE DOG
OELDBN	=	BLONDE
LLEWYO	=	YELLOW
KBCLA	=	BLACK
AOOCEHTCL	=	CHOCOLATE
UPPPY	=	PUPPY
NCAIEN	=	CANINE
9K	=	K9
RFUO EDEGGL	=	FOUR LEGGED
DOIF	=	FIDO

LET'S GO

IOVMES	=	MOVIES
GNKIIH	=	HIKING
LORLTS	=	STROLL
RRFBUSODA	=	SURFBOARD
IMTE FOF	=	TIME OFF
GSMNWIMI OOLP	=	SWIMMING POOL
IBRD TIAGWHNC	=	BIRD WATCHING
ADYOARWB	=	BROADWAY
SCBUIRONAL	=	BINOCULARS
GPIPNOSH	=	SHOPPING
EMOR	=	ROME
WNOS EOCN	=	SNOW CONE

MID-FALL

KHIGNI	=	HIKING
RECOSC	=	SOCCER
IAOGEFL	=	FOLIAGE
AKRE	=	RAKE
ACTECOLOH	=	CHOCOLATE
CCBPAKAK	=	BACKPACK
TTHISRSASWE	=	SWEATSHIRTS
TSVREAH	=	HARVEST
UMPPIKN	=	PUMPKIN
PALPE EPI	=	APPLE PIE
ESALPP	=	APPLES
ERDIHYA	=	HAYRIDE

CREATURES

OGDNAR	=	DRAGON
EBUL LEWAH	=	BLUE WHALE
ENAYH	=	HYENA
NRUNICO	=	UNICORN
NTUA	=	TUNA
LUYTPASP	=	PLATYPUS
STBASE	=	BASSET
DNHUO	=	HOUND
MISHPR	=	SHRIMP
KUSKN	=	SKUNK
OLDGULB	=	BULLDOG
DGALUYB	=	LADYBUG

POSITIVITY

ELRAEAEGB	=	AGREEABLE
ETANAIMD	=	ANIMATED
IRTGHB	=	BRIGHT
ERELVC	=	CLEVER
UNGECIRAGON	=	ENCOURAGING
HESFR	=	FRESH
ELETGN	=	GENTLE
EUHPOFL	=	HOPEFUL
IDKN	=	KIND
VNILGO	=	LOVING
PNOE	=	OPEN
SAEEDPL	=	PLEASED

SCARY STUFF

LNLAWEHOE	=	HALLOWEEN
YRCSA	=	SCARY
-KNJLATOECR-AN	=	JACK-O-LANTERN
TUDHNEA EHUSO	=	HAUNTED HOUSE
OSGHT YTOSR	=	GHOST STORY
IRSEPD	=	SPIDER
RLWEFOEW	=	WEREWOLF
ARCSY SEMOIV	=	SCARY MOVIES
DAVERRGYA	=	GRAVEYARD
INPMPUK	=	PUMPKIN
MAIPEVR	=	VAMPIRE
HMRAOMASWLL	=	MARSHMALLOW

SO BEAUTIFUL

ENIF	=	FINE
YXFO	=	FOXY
IGOOOLDNG-OK	=	GOOD-LOOKING
OGRSEUGO	=	GORGEOUS
RLFEAUGC	=	GRACEFUL
RANDG	=	GRAND
AMNOEDHS	=	HANDSOME
THO	=	HOT
YVOLEL	=	LOVELY
EMTNAFGICNI	=	MAGNIFICENT
UMEASRVLO	=	MARVELOUS
NTDRAAI	=	RADIANT

THANKSGIVING

YAMFLI	=	FAMILY
OINOCUPCRA	=	CORNUCOPIA
RSVETHA	=	HARVEST
LTLOFBOA	=	FOOTBALL
AHSQUS	=	SQUASH
OCIONKG	=	COOKING
TIEGAN	=	EATING
RCON	=	CORN
ELABT	=	TABLE
YRVGA	=	GRAVY
RRENRAYBC	=	CRANBERRY
GRMSLIIP	=	PILGRIMS

WATERS

OAYORR	=	ARROYO
ASINB	=	BASIN
YBA	=	BAY
YOUAB	=	BAYOU
EBDN	=	BEND
HIBTG	=	BIGHT
GBNOLBILA	=	BILLABONG
OGB	=	BOG
ROBOK	=	BROOK
LCAAN	=	CANAL
AACTARCT	=	CATARACT
ALNENCH	=	CHANNEL